Humor books available from InterVarsity Press

All God's Children Got Gum in Their Hair by Steve Phelps
Amusing Grace by Ed Koehler
As the Church Turns by Ed Koehler
Church Is Stranger Than Fiction by Mary Chambers
Climbing the Church Walls by Rob Portlock
Families Off the Wall by Rob Portlock
Faith in Orbit: A Spaced Odyssey by the IVP Cartoonists
It Came from Beneath the Pew by Rob Suggs
Less Than Entirely Sanctified by Doug Hall
Motherhood Is Stranger Than Fiction by Mary Chambers
Murphy Goes to Church by Steve Dennie and Rob Suggs
Murphy's Laws of Parenting by Steve Dennie and Rob Suggs
Reborn to Be Wild by Doug Hall
Off the Church Wall by Rob Portlock
101 Things to Do with a Dull Church by Martin Wroe and Adrian Reith
The Potluck Hall of Fame and Other Bizarre Christian Lists by David Dickerson and Mary Chambers
Preacher from the Black Lagoon by Rob Suggs
Way Off the Church Wall by Rob Portlock

Faith in Orbit
A Spaced Odyssey

by Mary Chambers, Doug Hall, Ed Koehler,
Rob Portlock & Rob Suggs

InterVarsity Press
Downers Grove, Illinois

InterVarsity Press® is the book-publishing division of InterVarsity Christian Fellowship®, a student movement active on campus at hundreds of universities, colleges and schools of nursing in the United States of America, and a member movement of the International Fellowship of Evangelical Students. For information about local and regional activities, write Public Relations Dept., InterVarsity Christian Fellowship, 6400 Schroeder Rd., P.O. Box 7895, Madison, WI 53707-7895.

Cover illustration: Rob Portlock with Mary Chambers, Doug Hall, Ed Koehler and Rob Suggs

ISBN 0-8308-1612-7

Printed in the United States of America ♾

Library of Congress Cataloging-in-Publication Data
Chambers, Mary.
   Faith in orbit: a spaced odyssey/Mary Chambers . . . [et al.].
     p.   cm.
   ISBN 0-8308-1612-7 (pbk.: alk. paper)
   1. Christian life—Caricatures and cartoons.   2. Christianity—
Forecasting—Caricatures and cartoons.   3. American wit and humor,
Pictorial.   I. Title.
BV4517.C43   1995
741.5'973—dc20   95-12633
                                   CIP

17	16	15	14	13	12	11	10	9	8	7	6	5	4	3	2	1
09	08	07	06	05	04	03	02	01	00	99	98	97	96	95		

Introduction

When Christianity Today, Inc., invited a crew of Christian cartoonists to Carol Stream for a convention, sensible publishers took cover. InterVarsity Press, however, invited five of these characters to come visit its offices. The so-called authors scribbled on our walls (okay, we put up some paper), mugged for a photo session and shamelessly promoted their books to the employees.

Since IVP was buying dinner, we thought the least the cartoonists could do was create a new book. This hilarious peek at what Christianity might look like in centuries to come is the result of their pooled brainpower.

What's it like to work with cartoonists? Well, aside from the fact that they think deadlines are the dates on which the editor will call to remind them to start working or the fact that most are physically incapable of conforming to a layout grid, it is a delight. These people are not just characters—they have *character*. You'll find that their sincere commitment to Christ and passion for his church shine through their work.

The best humor gives us glimpses of insight into ourselves and our world. And that's just what is in these pages.

The Editor

"Son, how about you and I having that little talk about, you know, genetic engineering."

PORTLOCK

MARCH 2015: E-MAILING-IN-TONGUES CRAZE SWEEPS TECHNO-CHARISMATIC MOVEMENT

"... BUT WE'VE *ALWAYS* HAD A DEACON IN CHARGE OF GROUNDS."

APRIL 2015: TENSION DEVELOPS BETWEEN THOSE INSISTING ON THE TRADITIONAL DISCO WORSHIP SERVICES, AND THE YOUNGER CROWD CALLING FOR TRENDIER GRUNGE WORSHIP

Millie Wilhelmia Cruikshank, age 3—
a reformation waiting in the wings.

HALL

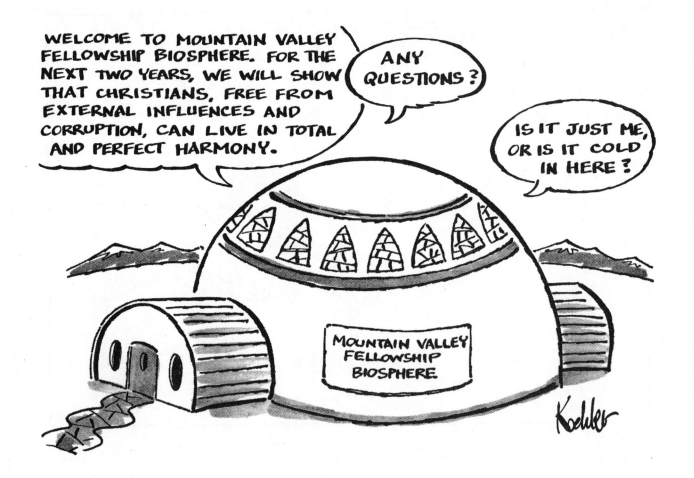

Bev Radcliff, Floral Pastor, 2020

"I don't care if it is 2025 . . . this church was built on its outreach to baby boomers and it's going to stay that way!"

"It'll be just a moment, Mr. Perkins. I'm having your life faxed over to me."

"WELL... THEY'VE FINALLY SEEN THROUGH THE DENOMINATION THING. NOW WHAT?"

"This gem was owned by a little gal who flew to Andromeda and back
to go to church on Sundays."

PORTLOCK

It was 2038 when the truth about what the first men on the moon really found came to light.

"Gotta run. You know how Frank gets when he's kept waiting in the teleporter."

MAY 2039: WITH 6,500 TV CHANNELS AVAILABLE, NEARLY EVERYONE CAN DO RELIGIOUS PROGRAMMING.

TELEVANGELISTS ON OTHER PLANETS

"...AND WITHOUT YOUR GIFT OF 25, 50 OR EVEN 100 CREDIT UNITS, THIS MINISTRY COULD SLIP INTO A BLACK HOLE."

chambers

"Looks like someone had a rough solar system crusade."

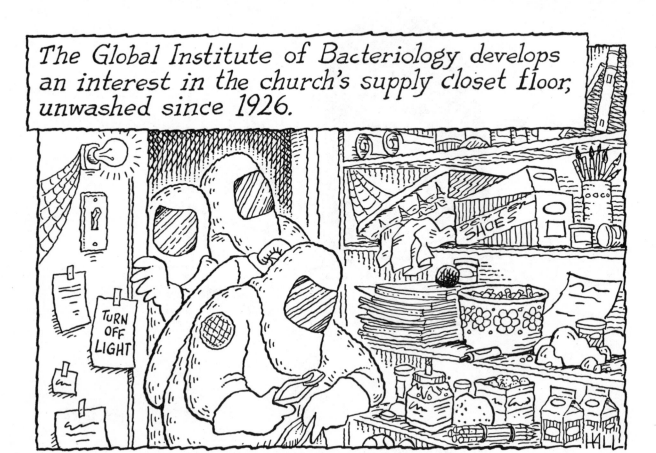

"Greta, come get a look at the new Youth Director!"

"I really enjoy living on the moon, but could you do something about the Tang?"

Christian publishers target increasingly specialized audiences.

CERTAIN THAT THE SECOND COMING CAN'T BE LONG NOW, AND
FACED WITH THE PROSPECTS OF ANOTHER ELECTION YEAR,
BOB AND NELLIE CHAMBERS OF SCOTTDALE, PA, DECIDE THEY'LL JUST WAIT.

First Sunday-school class on the moon.

IN THE FUTURE, SOME CHURCHES ABUSE
CHURCH GROWTH TECHNIQUES...

"We'd be delighted to have you in our church and are offering a package of $75,000.00 per year, plus expenses. We do prefer you attend regularly, and we don't apologize for it."

WHILE OTHERS ARE QUITE SUCCESSFUL AT AVOIDING THE "NUMBERS GAME"...

"Of course if it's a country club you're looking for, you can join the 225-member church down the road with their *user friendly*, indoor pu-u-lumbing-ah!!"

MARCH 2056: SNEAKY NEW WITNESSING STRATEGIES

"YOU KNOW, MOST BIBLICAL SCHOLARS NOW AGREE THAT THE WHOLE QUESTION OF RIGHT AND WRONG WAS A CULTURAL THING."

Upon serving its 50 millionth customer, Happy Hank's House of Prayer franchise chain becomes the nation's largest denomination.

"Please take the instruction card in front of you and follow along as the flight attendants go through the FAA safety instructions."

ADVANCES IN HEALTH CARE CHANGES THE FACE OF YOUTH GROUPS.

"I just love it when the choir does that."

"Fine sermon, Reverend, and I really admire your medieval vestments."

"MY CLIENT HAS A RIGHT TO SEE ANY EVIDENCE
GOD MAY USE AGAINST HIM IN ANY FUTURE COURT ACTION."

EARL'S
CATHOLIC CHAPEL,
BAPTIST CHURCH,
AND
WASH & LUBE

Declining rural populations require institutional consolidation.

"Here's an idea for the next senior-high lock-in. This here is the church Biosphere!"

Sparkle Window Cleaner's board of directors celebrate getting the account
of the one hundred Crystal Cathedrals.

The Retro-Church Movement finds comfort in reliving the 1950s.

"ARCHAEOLOGICAL EVIDENCE SEEMS TO SUGGEST THAT EARTH WAS TAKEN OVER BY THESE CREATURES OF APPARENT SUPERIOR BRAIN CAPACITY BUT WHOSE MOVEMENT WAS HAMPERED BY EXCESSIVE FOOT SIZE AND THE FACT THAT THEY WERE GENERALLY GLUED TO A BASE OR PEDESTAL OF SOME SORT."

"Your prayer life looks good, devotionals look great, quiet time is average. But, boy, your tithing is back in the twentieth century!"

"That, in a nutshell, is truth as I perceive it. Why don't you share truth as you perceive it, and then we'll settle on a middle-ground truth as both perceive it."

"Jones family, you are cleared for landing on lot eleven . . . Nelsons, hold your pattern, please . . .
Ms. Olson, you are cleared for landing on lot six . . ."

BUS KIDS

JUNE 2180: PLANET NEPTUNE TP'ED BY THE YOUTH GROUP

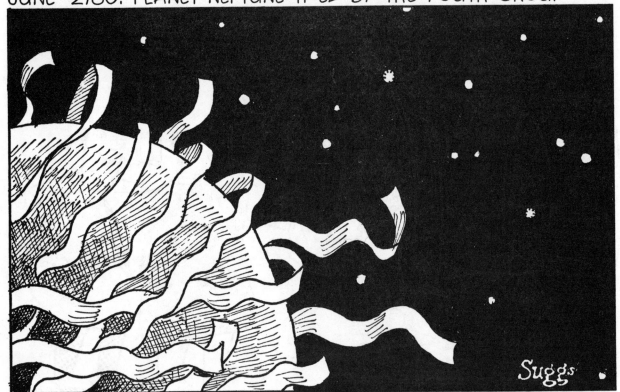

Suggs

"Just wait. Someday somebody will trash us for interfering with their local customs."

PORTLOCK

"I kinda miss the good ol' days when we had pews."

Spinoff churches of the future.

"OKAY! WE'VE SAVED THE WHALE, THE SPOTTED OWL, THE RAINFOREST, THE BALD EAGLE, THE SNAIL DARTER AND THE DOLPHINS. DID WE FORGET ANYBODY?"

"I think it's safe to say who the first-time visitors are."

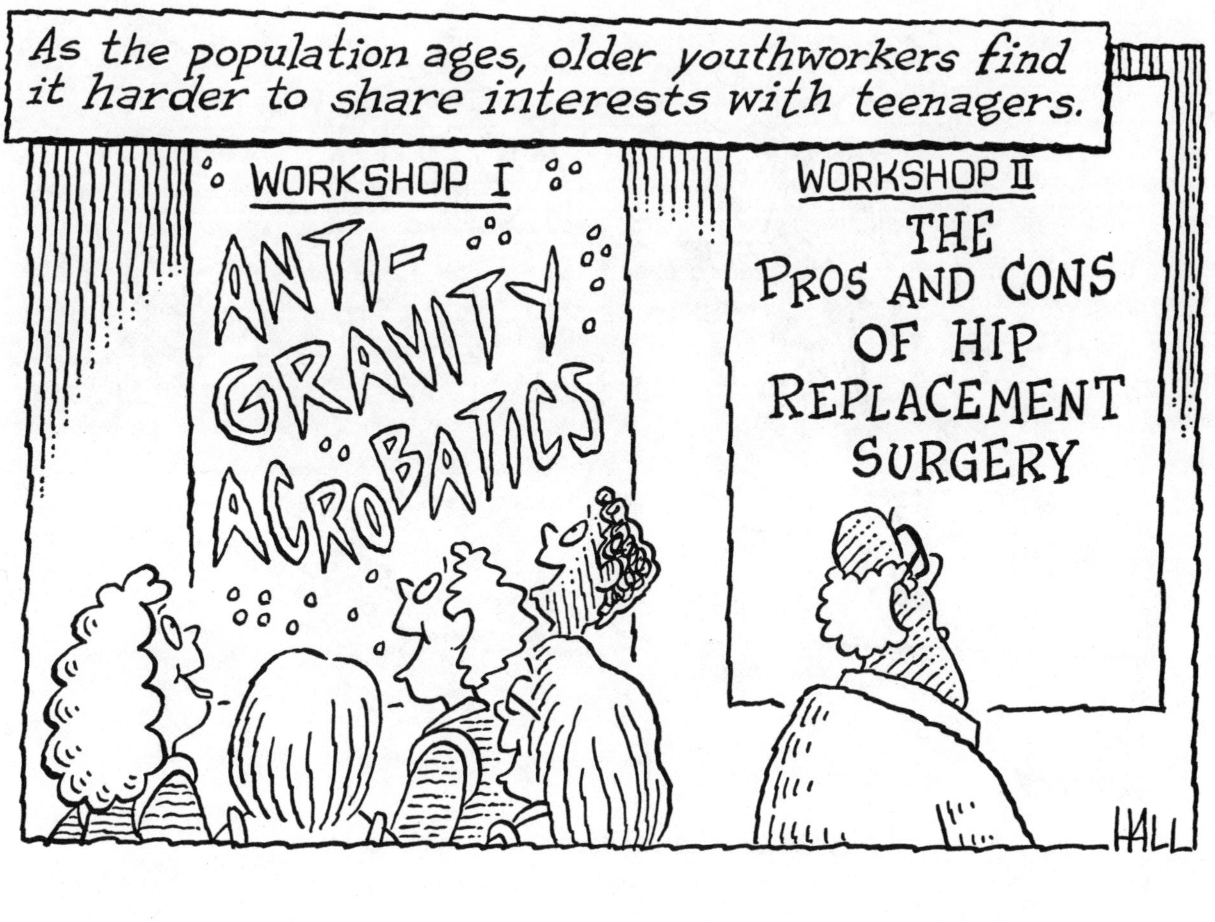
As the population ages, older youthworkers find it harder to share interests with teenagers.
WORKSHOP I
ANTI-GRAVITY ACROBATICS
WORKSHOP II
THE PROS AND CONS OF HIP REPLACEMENT SURGERY
HALL

The model 4000 tithe collector was a complete bust.

The happy union of technology and accountability.

"WELL, AT LEAST YOU'RE NOT DATING SOMEONE FROM ANOTHER DENOMINATION!"

January 1, 2290: The Mormons go intergalactic.

By 2302 differences become less of an issue in some churches . . .

... and more of an issue in others.

In 2416 a harsher view is taken of those late for church.

DRESSED FOR MOBILITY; OUTFITTING THE *21ST* CENTURY PASTOR

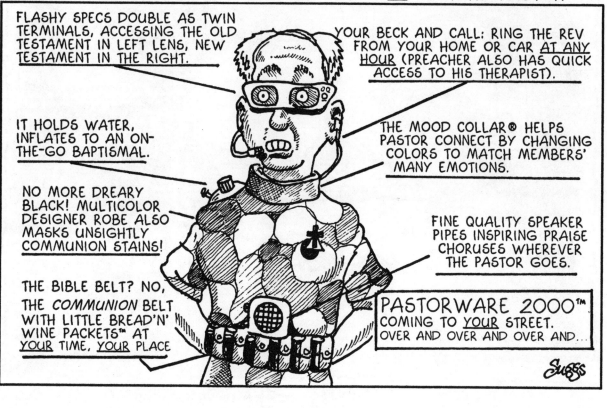

FLASHY SPECS DOUBLE AS TWIN TERMINALS, ACCESSING THE OLD TESTAMENT IN LEFT LENS, NEW TESTAMENT IN THE RIGHT.

YOUR BECK AND CALL: RING THE REV FROM YOUR HOME OR CAR <u>AT ANY HOUR</u> (PREACHER ALSO HAS QUICK ACCESS TO HIS THERAPIST).

IT HOLDS WATER, INFLATES TO AN ON-THE-GO BAPTISMAL.

THE MOOD COLLAR® HELPS PASTOR CONNECT BY CHANGING COLORS TO MATCH MEMBERS' MANY EMOTIONS.

NO MORE DREARY BLACK! MULTICOLOR DESIGNER ROBE ALSO MASKS UNSIGHTLY <u>COMMUNION STAINS!</u>

FINE QUALITY SPEAKER PIPES INSPIRING PRAISE CHORUSES WHEREVER THE PASTOR GOES.

THE BIBLE BELT? NO, THE *COMMUNION* BELT WITH LITTLE BREAD'N' WINE PACKETS™ AT <u>YOUR</u> TIME, <u>YOUR</u> PLACE

PASTORWARE 2000™ COMING TO <u>YOUR</u> STREET. OVER AND OVER AND OVER AND...

Suggs

"AHA! JUST AS I THOUGHT — CHANNEL SURFING ON THE INTERACTIVE POT LUCK NETWORK AGAIN!"

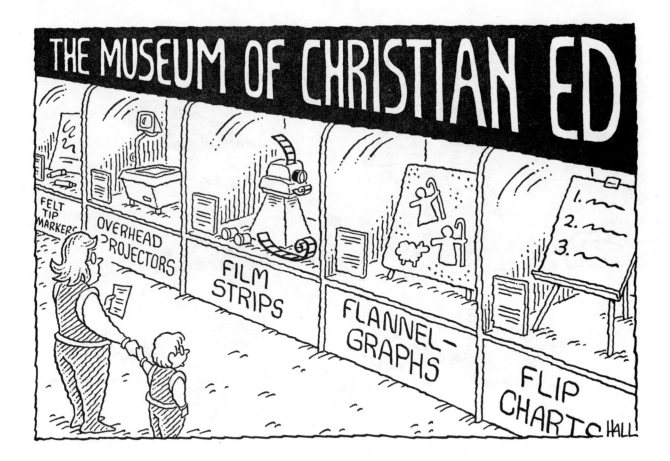

"Well, I see the Newburys brought their same old B-12 Complex."

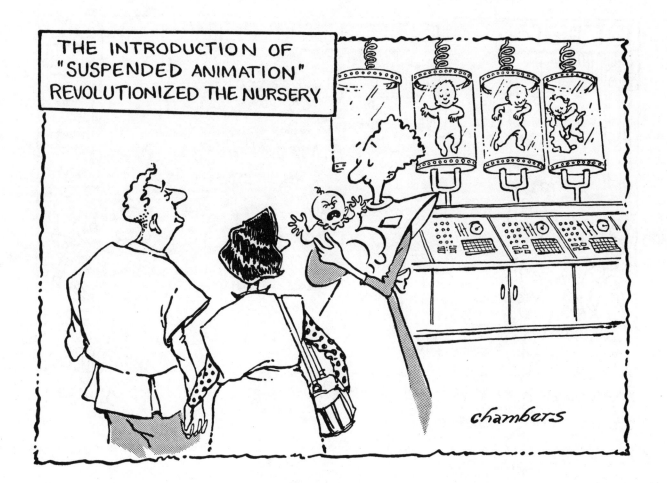

The church's chronic volunteer shortage was solved by the cloning of Jeanette.

"Now with every head bowed and every—pew 27105G, please bow your head!"

EVENTUALLY EVEN CERTAIN MODERN TRENDS IN WORSHIP HAD BECOME FORMALIZED

chambers

"...AND NOW WHILE OUR BAND PLAYS, LET US RAISE OUR HANDS AND SING VERSES 1,2 & 4 SIXTY-TWO TIMES, FALLING PROSTRATE ON THE LAST STANZA FOR PRAYER."

Church growth consultants recommend padding small congregations with holograms.

DATE UNKNOWN: END TIMES PROPHETS FINALLY RUN OUT OF PREDICTIONS AND GET A LIFE, JUST AS ACTUAL RAPTURE OCCURS

"IT IS ESTIMATED THAT THE UNITED STATES SANK ANOTHER 2.6 FEET THIS WEEK UNDER THE CRUSHING WEIGHT OF ACCUMULATED UNUSED SUNDAY SCHOOL CURRICULUM."

"Late 20th century, American . . . rectangular Pyrex, 9 × 13, hard wheat noodle remnants, dried cheese from cow's milk. This has something to do with religion."

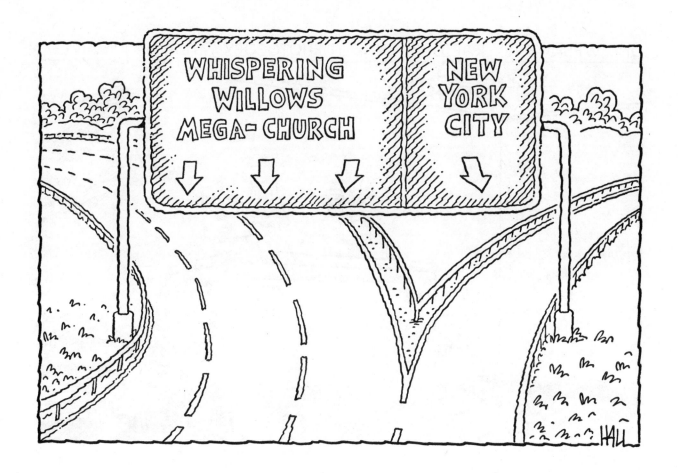